A CHILD'S STORY OF JESUS

Barbara Kanaar
illustrated by Jan Rice

STANDARD
PUBLISHING

The Standard Publishing Company, Cincinnati, Ohio
A division of Standex International Corporation
©1992 by The Standard Publishing Company
All rights reserved.
Printed in the United States of America
01 00 99 98 97 96 95 94   5 4 3 2 1

Third Edition, 1994
Library of Congress Catalog Card No. 91-46808
ISBN 0-7847-0267-5

Designed by Coleen Davis

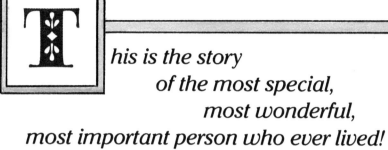

This is the story
of the most special,
most wonderful,
most important person who ever lived!

Jesus was born one night long ago in the little town of Bethlehem, in a stable where cows and donkeys were kept. Mary and Joseph loved baby Jesus. Mary wrapped Him in soft cloths and laid Him in a manger filled with clean hay.

Luke 2:1-7

LOOK inside the stable.
Find baby Jesus sleeping.
Point to His little manger bed.
Where is Mary?
Can you find Joseph?
Point to all the animals.
Can you count them?
Can you name each one?

appy shepherds came to see baby Jesus. An angel had told them where to find Him. The shepherds thanked God for sending His Son and for letting them be the first to see Him.   *Luke 2:8-20*

LOOK out in the fields.
Where are the shepherds?
Where are their sheep?
Point to the stars in the sky.
Can you find the angel?
What did the angel say?

Jesus' next visitors were wise men from a faraway land. A special, sparkling star led them to the right house. Jesus was now a little boy. The wise men gave Him presents, and they thanked God for sending His Son.

Matthew 2:1-12

LOOK inside the little house.
Where is Jesus?
Can you find Mary?
Point to the wise men.
Count their presents.
Do you see a camel?
Where is the sparkling star?

**M**ary and Joseph and Jesus moved to the town of Nazareth. Joseph was a carpenter. He made things out of wood. When Jesus was a boy, He helped Joseph in the carpentry shop.   *Matthew 2:19-23*

LOOK inside the carpentry shop.
Can you find two saws?
Point to Joseph's hammer.
What is Jesus holding?
Can you find some blocks?
Do you see a toy top?
Can you find a wooden stool?
Where is the kitten in a basket?

When Jesus became a man, He began to tell people everywhere about His Father, God. He called some men to be disciples, His special helpers. Some of Jesus' disciples were fishermen. *Mark 1:14-20; 3:13-19*

LOOK at the seashore.
Where are the fishermen?
Can you count them?
Where is Jesus?
Point to the fish.
Point to the boats.
Do you see some sea gulls?

Jesus fell asleep in a boat on the lake. When a storm began, Jesus' disciples woke Him up because they were afraid. "Calm down, waves," said Jesus. "Stop blowing, wind." Right away, the wind and waves obeyed. Only Jesus could stop a storm! *Luke 8:22-25*

LOOK at the lake.
Where is the boat?
Point to the clouds.
Where is the lightning?
Do you see the waves?
Point to Jesus.
What is Jesus telling the wind?
What is He telling the waves?

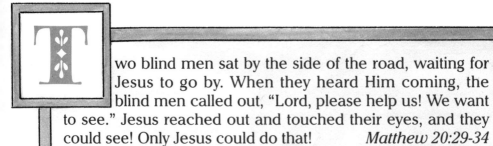

Two blind men sat by the side of the road, waiting for Jesus to go by. When they heard Him coming, the blind men called out, "Lord, please help us! We want to see." Jesus reached out and touched their eyes, and they could see! Only Jesus could do that!   *Matthew 20:29-34*

LOOK at the roadside.
Where are the blind men?
Point to their eyes.
Who made the blind men see?
Point to Jesus.

ne day Jesus rode into a city on a little donkey. Happy people walked in front of Him, and happy people walked behind Him. Everyone was singing and waving palm branches. What a parade for Jesus! *Matthew 21:1-11*

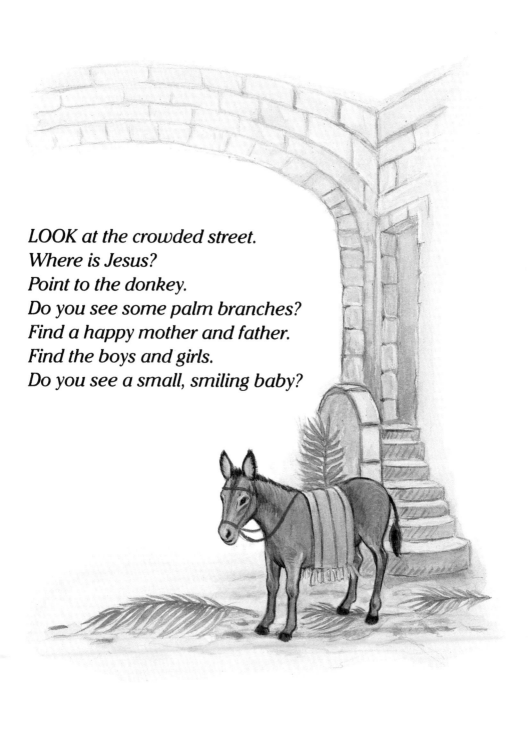

LOOK at the crowded street.
Where is Jesus?
Point to the donkey.
Do you see some palm branches?
Find a happy mother and father.
Find the boys and girls.
Do you see a small, smiling baby?

 ot everyone loved Jesus. One day a sad thing happened—Jesus was killed on a cross by people who didn't love Him. Jesus' friends laid His body in a tomb. But God made Jesus alive again! An angel at the tomb said, "Jesus is not here. He is risen!"   *Luke 23:33—24:49*

LOOK inside the empty tomb.
Jesus isn't there! Jesus is alive!
Point to Jesus.
Find the women.
Where is the angel?
What did the angel say?

I t was time for Jesus to go home to Heaven. "Go everywhere and tell everyone about me," He told His disciples. Then He went up into the sky on a cloud. An angel came and told the disciples that Jesus will come back someday. What a wonderful promise! The disciples told everyone they met about Jesus, God's Son—the most special, most wonderful, most important person who ever lived.

Matthew 28:18-20;
Luke 24:50-53; Acts 1:9-11

LOOK at the sky.
Point to the clouds.
Where is Jesus?
Where is Jesus going?
Point to the disciples.
Do they look surprised?
Do they look happy?
Will Jesus come back someday?